MOTIVATIONAL QUOTES TO GET THE BLOOD MOVING.

Markus Almond

CONTENTS:

INTRODUCTION.

Motivational Quotes To Get The Blood Moving is for people who would like to do extraordinary things with their lives. If you ever feel stuck or stagnant, like you're working too hard and going no where, this book is for you. It's for those who want to be happy, make a fortune or do something creative. It's for anyone who wants to start a business, get in shape or just work less and spend more time with family.

A few years ago, I started writing books as a way to motivate myself. I wrote things that I could look back on when I was feeling stressed or lost - little reminders to help me stay on track. It started to work almost immediately. I wrote about will power and quit smoking. I wrote about money and doubled my income. I got married, started a business and reached the Amazon best-seller list with one of my poetry books.

But my motivational quotes weren't just working for me, they were also having an impact on other artists out there making their dreams a reality. Some of the biggest names in entertainment started to share my motivational quotes. Travis Barker from Blink-182, posted my work on Instagram and said it was, "Inspiring and Motivating." Rob

Dyrdek, who was producing and starring in the most successful shows on MTV posted photos of my work and said it was, "One of the best reads about life and success that I have read in a long time."

The most rewarding aspect of what I do are the emails I get from people just starting out - messages from small business owners or young girls starting a band and going into the recording studio for the first time. I started on this journey as a songwriter in a punk band who's songs have appeared on MTV, the E! Network and other networks. So when someone tells me that my books have inspired them to start a business or join a band I get very excited. Those emails and messages are what keeps me going.

I hope this book has a great impact on your life. Trust these words and bring them with you on all your adventures. I'm here if you need anything.

-Markus Almond

· Part One ·

MISTAKES

Welcome to the world. You will hurt
the people you love the most. You will
say stupid things and embarrass yourself
repeatedly. You will crash your car and
lose your wallet before the bill comes.
You will get sick, sad and lonely. You'll
oversleep on the day of the big meeting.
But there are wonderful things in this world
too. And the dumb mistakes that make us
human are just a sneeze on your wedding day.
They are just one bad peanut in a Payday
bar. They are just a stubbed toe on the way
to the best sex of your life.

Learning to fail is an important part of success. I'd like everyone reading this to fail at something. Get out there and try the impossible. Set your sights high and do something that you're almost certain is beyond your skill level. Call the girl. Meet with a millionaire. Pitch your art project to a retail store. Negotiate a large salary increase. Push yourself to accomplish something enormous. You may fail a hundred times. But it only takes one success to completely change your life.

The most valuable lessons we will ever learn are the ones that happen after we fall flat on our faces without anyone around to catch us.

Mistakes are a natural byproduct of personal growth. They are tied to success like the broken egg of a newborn eaglet or a pile of rocks under an exquisite sculpture.

Refusing to take risks will dull the shine right out of your life. Be brave enough to be vulnerable. Be smart enough to let your fears melt into extraordinary capabilities.

We will make mistakes. We will fall in love
with the wrong people, apply for the wrong
jobs and leave our houses when we should
have just stayed home. We will score low
on tests, fail miserably during important
challenges. We will have to reconsider our
future and our careers on several occasions.
But the days that come when our loved ones
are happy and everything is going right –
those are the days we live for. And there
will be plenty of them to come when we're
not embarrassed to fail.

Call someone right now and ask them for something ridiculous. Call the credit card company and ask them to wipe your balance clean. Call your favorite restaurant and ask if they'd be willing to offer you a free meal. Get used to asking for the unreasonable. Get comfortable with ridiculous expectations. You'll find that once you develop this skill, you'll accomplish things you never thought possible.

It's important to keep going. You will fall sometimes and that's normal. Just don't let things paralyze you. Don't worry about making sense of your blunder. Forget it and move on.

If you're operating at a 20% success rate, you will succeed. If you keep pushing through even in the face of rejection, you will succeed. If you're smart enough to readjust when you hit a wall without dwelling on misfortune, you will succeed. If you believe in yourself and the goodness of the world, you will succeed.

Here's the thing about mistakes. No one is paying attention. No one knows you're making mistakes but you. Call attention to them and everyone will call you a fuck up. Move on and no one will know the difference.

Ignore your failures. Your subconscious got it and won't forget. It's all in there for next time. You don't need to dwell on that shit on a conscious level.

WE HURT EACH OTHER BECAUSE WE'RE FLAWED. WE FORGIVE EACH OTHER BECAUSE WE'RE BEAUTIFUL.

You can't look back, really. The best you can do is try not to make the same mistakes moving forward. Rejection is just another word for "still working on it."

The most successful people in America know a thousand times more about defeat and failure than any poor fool who quit after a couple of rejection letters.

Getting comfortable with rejection is just
a part of success. Find what works for you.
Get angry. Construct a mask and keep your
emotions out of it. Do what you've got
to do. But dance with rejection because
there are a million opportunities out there
if you're brave enough to make yourself
vulnerable.

We've got to love rejection. We've got to eat the stuff for breakfast. Rejection is a temporary and unimportant hurdle. It's just a dusty wall between two open doors.

Disregard your rejections. They vanish from history and years from now, you'll appear to be an overnight success.

No one ever said you had to be perfect. No one ever said you weren't supposed to be nervous. No one said that you had to do it like everyone else. No one said that you weren't allowed to stumble over your words or laugh inappropriately. We are only human and we should love ourselves for that.

YOU CAN'T IMPROVE YOUR LIFE WITHOUT TRYING SOMETHING NEW.

Most people tend to sell themselves short and aim too low. The world is a lot more elastic and conquerable than most people realize. Just try things. You'll see reality bend and twist. You'll see the cracks of opportunity reveal themselves in the status quo. You'll see the weak points and the way to break through to the other side.

Push it forward. Imagine that anything is possible and push it all the way to the top. If you want to make money, start 5 little businesses and see what happens. If you want a girlfriend, ask 5 girls out. If you want to push your art forward, do 5 things to help it succeed. You only have to be right 20% of the time to get what you want.

All the successful people you see, all
those high-rollers that you keep comparing
yourself to, they've all been through hell.
They've all been beat up, knocked down and
told they're no good. Every one of them
has had their heart broken and their dreams
stepped on. But they got up again. They
seem different because they don't dwell.
They seem more successful because they don't
let their failures define them. Concentrate
on the good in your life and keep trying.

There will be plenty of people waiting to
kick you in the junk. Wear a cup when you
leave the house and smile at the bastards.
They lose all their power when they realize
they have no effect on you.

Successful people have a knack for ignoring hurtful criticism. They welcome feedback and adapt. They make slight adjustments when necessary. But they never internalize negative opinions and they know the difference between an error in judgment and a lack of character.

Choose to be impressed with life again. Be
amazed by the ordinary. Love everybody
because everybody tries. And love yourself
because you're the lens that makes all this
beauty possible in the first place.

Be comfortable with confrontation. Go talk to someone and say something controversial. Put yourself in situations where you can dance in conflict. The more experienced and comfortable you are with conflict, the better equipped you'll be for controlling situations that actually matter.

Don't tell me that you can't do it or that you never learned BLAH or you don't have the qualifications for BLAH. Put your shoes on and go down to where the people are. Pick up the phone and be brave enough to make a fool of yourself. I swear to you with everything that is holy, if you just have the stubbornness to call 10 or 20 people, one of them will change your life.

LET US ALL BE BRAVE OR STUPID ENOUGH TO ASK HIGH LEVEL DECISION MAKERS TO MAKE US BUSINESS PARTNERS AND TO ALWAYS DATE PEOPLE OUT OF OUR LEAGUE.

Never be too realistic to try something new.
Never be too experienced to fall in love.
Keep an open heart and an open mind and be
willing to let both of them rip open and
destroy you if necessary. It isn't long now
until we'll all be buried in the ground.

Try everything. Don't be afraid to
quit. Be nimble. Get as much feedback as
possible. Remember, if one out of five
people are giving you a chance, your odds of
success are awesome. You only need to try
100 times to have 20 successful projects.

Life doesn't always turn out the way we hope or expect. But as long as we have a working imagination, we can find a way to succeed. Reassess and proceed with courage.

We're capable of enduring a great deal of pain and bullshit. We should do a better job of lowering our tolerance for such things. We should all be quicker to get the hell out of situations that are doing the world no good.

Don't quit because it's hard. Quit because
you have better options than when you
started.

In finance they call it "diversifying your portfolio" but in art you should try to have many projects cooking at the same time. This increases your chances of success. If one project starts to get momentum, put all your energy into pushing it forward. Let go of the duds and concentrate on what works.

Quitting isn't always permanent. For things that were meant to be, you can go back.

Condors have to learn to fly. World
champions were once amateurs. Let's
flounder. Let's be inexperienced and
awkward and lets be brave enough to keep
trying.

We usually don't do what we're told. We're
not afraid to use our imaginations and force
a fresh path through the wilderness. We're
not afraid of making mistakes or changing
course. We are nimble and always one step
ahead of our competition.

You've got to learn to take risks. Be proud of looking like a complete idiot once in a while. There are many kinds of growth and all of them require that you abandon safety and comfort long enough to learn something new.

Sometimes we don't have the tools we need to love somebody properly. Sometimes it takes failure and an earth-shattering disaster to give us the insight that we need to get our shit together.

Sometimes our weaknesses become our strengths. "He's insecure about himself. But I think that's what drives him to be so good at what he does," she said.

Not all of us are perfect. But I find that the people out there making the greatest mistakes are also the most passionate and lovely people that I have known.

We can rewrite the past. We can reinvent
ourselves. We turn can turn tragedy into
romance. And we can always turn devastation
into spiritual enlightenment.

Start again. Just shake yourself off like a wet dog, jump in there and start again.

- Part Two -

Money is important for pursuing dreams.
You can't write the great American novel
if you're stuck at some job for 70 hours
a week. Money is one way to comfortably
redirect our attention to things we're
passionate about. It is a useful tool.
This is all. The important thing is not to
feel guilty when you start making a lot of
money.

You can be a millionaire without being
a jerk. You can own your own business
in a non-stressful way. You can do yoga
and find daily peace even as your monthly
income triples. Wealth can change your bank
account without affecting who you are and
how you love.

There is a technique that will almost
always improve your life. Help people and
solve problems. Do anything you can to add
value in these ways. Find out what people
want and give it to them. Exceed their
expectations.

Money doesn't have to be dirty. We get
to decide how money is acquired and used.
We get to define the rules. We can work
together without competing. We can invent
a game together and we can both win. Maybe
the game today is "Working in the garden."
I'm pretty good at raking and pulling weeds.
You're pretty good at picking vegetables.
We get to play our own games and work on
being the best versions of ourselves. And
we both get to eat a good meal. This works
for money too. My goal might be "to provide
as much value today as possible and to pay
my rent by the end of the week." You could
have the same goal. But because no two
people provide the same kind of value, we
can BOTH meet our goals.

If you can structure your life around helping others, if you can find a way to love what you're doing, you will be wealthy, happy and healthy. If you can find a way to improve the lives of the people around you, wonderful things will fall into place.

There is value everywhere – value in your knowledge and skills, talents and passions. Wealth comes from recognizing this value and working hard to convert it into mutually beneficial relationships. Reach out to more people. Be resourceful. Be inventive.

Stop focusing on what you want and start focusing on what you can give. Concentrate on what you can offer to the good people of the world. Perfect that gift.

Look for ways to help people out before they even realize that they need help. Be the source of something magnificent that cannot be replaced.

Success is built with mutual beneficial circumstances. Let your fans, customers and partners leave every experience feeling like they got more than they bargained for. Both of you can feel this way. It's one of the miracles of the universe.

Create something extraordinary.

Let money be a tool of peace and freedom.

You don't have to worship material things
or succumb to greed. If you can adapt the
belief that your skills are highly valued,
the universe will pay you accordingly. And
when the time comes, you can do really great
things with that currency.

We cannot feed hungry people by refusing to eat.

Concentrate on making the best use of your energy. Concentrate on structuring a life that allows you to offer something really incredible to the world. Set up a work life where you are able to leverage your talents and create amazing things.

Success is just a new spring jacket after
the last freeze has thawed.

We are a species of animals living
peacefully on the planet. Your I.Q. doesn't
matter. Your body type or race doesn't
matter. Your ability to get along with
the other humans determines your place in
society. Be happy and confident enough to
know that you are a very important member
of the community. Be thankful because you
deserve to be rewarded for such value.
Treat everyone well and things will be good
for you.

Money doesn't have to create distance
between our friends and the people we love.
It doesn't have to make things weird. Money
is just a thing. It's just a number in a
bank account. It is there for emergencies
or family vacations. It is there for the
people we love. We can bring money into our
lives without letting it change us.

WE'VE GOT TO BE OKAY WITH THE FACT THAT WE CAN HAVE INSANELY LARGE AMOUNTS OF CASH IN OUR BANK ACCOUNTS.

People who appear to be an overnight success have been working for years. They've been making mistakes and learning about themselves. They've been studying their craft and trying to understand how to help people. They've been perfecting their product and improving their capabilities.

Let us love the successful people. Let us feel joy and pride for them. In doing this, we expunge all envy and feelings of jealousy from our gut. When we can feel genuine happiness for those who live with wealth, we welcome it into our own lives.

There are so many opportunities to create
personal wealth. The challenge is to
confront our inner consciousness. The
challenge is to observe and overcome the
thoughts that restrict us.

The universe acts like a large terrifying,
dog that can destroy you at any moment. It
is very receptive and always listening.
Tell the dog to sit and it will sit. Tell
the dog to shake hands and it will offer you
its paw. Run away frantically and it will
chase you down the block and bite you. The
dog doesn't know what's happening. It just
wants to play your game. We don't want to
admit this simple fact. We don't like to
play with animals that can destroy us. We
don't want to shake hands with something
that has that kind of power. So we try to
take its power away. We tell ourselves that
the universe isn't really listening. We
tell ourselves that things are random. And
the universe shows us what we expect to see.

Attempting to acquire something by
definition establishes you as someone who
is lacking. When you realize that you have
everything you need, you will encourage
further abundance.

Wealth is a vortex of spinning energy. It's powerful but not dangerous. It is alive but means us no harm. It can grow, vanish or multiply but it does not determine our worth. Wealth appears for those willing to accept the responsibility.

Sometimes all you have to do is ask. Ask your boss for a raise. Ask a high roller for some support. A very famous musician tweeted a photo of my book the other day. I didn't do anything to deserve that. I just found his address online and sent him a book. These things aren't difficult. It just takes a little optimism and work.

Money allows a man to spend his days with oil paints. Money allows a man to write novels uninterrupted.

Money is morally neutral. The power of
capital is decided by its owner. FOUR
HUNDRED AND FIFTY THOUSAND DOLLARS is just a
line in the sand.

Sometimes we don't want the responsibility of abundance. We worry that if we have something it may be lost or taken away. But you should know that once you learn how to acquire something, it becomes very easy to acquire it again.

Let us always be thankful and never feel guilty for making more money than our parents.

Be happy for those who have, and you will open yourself to a life of abundance.

One kind of currency can be converted into another. American dollars can be converted to Euros. Time and energy can be converted too. But the beauty of energy is that YOU determine how it is converted. You get to decide how much your energy is worth.

FIND A THING THAT YOU'RE GOOD AT. DEVOTE YOUR LIFE TO IT.

This is all a game. And that game should be fun. It's okay to fail. But you've got to try. That first step is all it takes. After you try it once, it becomes easier to try again. You may fail the first time but you will learn an infinite amount of things that can be applied to many different facets of life. You will learn how to carry yourself and persevere until you bring spiritual and physical wealth into your life.

Stop wondering whether your idea is a good idea and go try it out.

We do this thing in our lives. We talk ourselves out of it. We say, "Well, even if I went back to school and got a degree, who knows if I'd even get a job in that field." Or "Yeah, I'd like to quit my job but I'm lucky to even have a job in this economy. If I work somewhere else, they might fire me or take away my benefits or blah." It's just a little touch of fear. It can be overcome. It should be overcome. It is waiting to be overcome whenever you're ready.

If you're stuck and things aren't working,
there is a good chance that you're not
confronting something. I know that can
be terrifying. But it is worth trying to
figure out. It is worth it to be honest
with yourself and have a good cry. It
is a wonderful investment to really
understand yourself and come to a problem or
opportunity with a clear perspective.

I stopped playing music for a few reason.
One of those reasons was because there
were many other bands doing what I was
trying to do. Not to get into a lesson
about economics, but the market place was
saturated with similar products. And I
wasn't able to distinguish myself in a way
that provided more value than the other
guys. The best thing I did was quit. If
you find yourself in a place where there is
a ton of competition and no inherent way of
setting yourself apart, you should get out
of there. People need to be excited about
what you're doing. Find something that
excites people.

Listen to your customers. What do they want more of? What are they willing to pay for? Try things. See what works. Focus your energy on the transactions that are bringing you value. If you work for someone else, your most important customer is your boss. What can you do to make yourself irreplaceable?

To provide value, you must be empathetic
and sensitive to other peoples needs. You
must be willing to try things and be okay
with failure. You must see through the eyes
of the customer. Look at yourself from the
outside.

Making money always starts with a positive attitude.

The best you can do is devote your energy
to something you love doing. If you find
that you are good at something, keep doing
it. Building wealth is a slow and grueling
process. Increase your worth one day at a
time. The worst thing you can do is stop
trying. Change if you must but don't give
up.

Good luck moves like a thousand glowing
fish, they dance in unison and can be easily
spooked. Be still and keep your breath
steady. Welcome luck into your life and
don't flinch when it arrives.

Visualization alone doesn't work. What works is improving your capabilities and pushing yourself to be brave. What works is acquiring new skills and being aggressive about creating opportunities. What works is convincing yourself that you're worthy of being happy. What works is being emotionally and psychologically okay with the idea of having money.

If you refuse to take no for an answer, if
you only take opportunities that lead you to
your ultimate goal, the universe will have
no choice but to take you where you want to
go.

See if you can play with money and create
more. Don't "spend" money. Trade it for
things that are worth more. Don't spend a
dime. Your transactions should always be
mutually beneficial. Sacrifice is giving up
one thing for something that is worth much
more. Never think of spending money as a
dead end. If it doesn't add value to your
life, don't buy it.

One of the most common mistakes a young artist can make is to overspend on promotion. This is especially common for those who are overconfident. They hire a big league publicist for a mediocre product. They spend 4 months of grocery money on advertising. This is a rookie mistake that can be avoided. You will be approached by many qualified agencies trying to sell you the dream. Save your money. Don't spend yourself into failure.

The important thing is to hold on. Don't get desperate. Don't give up hope. We control where we go next. Don't worry about what other people have. Look inward. You will see a wealth of possibilities with the right set of eyes.

Remember, the way to sustain a good living
is to offer something of value and to make
good trades. Stay away from debt because
it promises energy and value that you do not
yet possess. Make good on promises before
creating new ones. Be skeptical of hourly
wages.

There are universal laws that they don't
teach in school. Most schools teach people
how to compete for the same jobs - jobs
where you have to viciously compete with co-
workers and learn how to smile at people you
don't like and laugh at jokes that aren't
funny. They teach people how to eat shit
and follow the rules. But it doesn't have
to be that way. If spiritual suffocation
was the only way to make money, I would be
the poorest man on earth. Things don't
work that way. There are wonderful jobs
and opportunities out there. Things are
a thousand times easier if you provide
value to the world in a way no one else has
thought of before.

We've got to get used to the idea that we can take a very long vacation and still come home with plenty of cash for several more vacations.

BE BOLD ENOUGH TO RAISE THE STANDARDS OF EVERYONE AROUND YOU.

- Part Three -

TRUE SELF

Let's be preposterous. Let's be ridiculous. Let's be utterly oblivious to what is expected of us. Let's change everything and really drop the jaws of bystanders. Let's break every rule not out of spite but out of necessity and dedication to the bigger picture.

THE CHOICE IS SIMPLE. YOU CAN EITHER EMBRACE YOUR TRUE SELF OR BE A SECOND-RATE VERSION OF SOMEBODY ELSE.

Let me tell you about what drives me. I wanted to stay up all night working on projects that I was proud of - projects that I was passionate about. And why shouldn't I be able to do these things? Why shouldn't YOU be able to do these things? This chapter is about staying true to ourselves. It is about loving who we are and what we're good at. Do this and amazing things will happen for you.

If you want to blaze your own path you've
got to be friends with the dark and
dangerous stuff inside you. You've got to
be friends with your emotions and know when
to back off and when to fight through. You
will get to know your inner self intimately.
This happens when you face difficulties
and problems and adversity in the external
world. Eventually, the only thing left
holding you back is yourself.

Failure just means you stop when things aren't going well. Success means finding a way to sustain, grow, or evolve. Birds can fly because they have hallow bones. Fish can swim because their gills absorb the oxygen from water. Artists can sleep late in the mornings because they learned when to compromise and when to stay the course.

Believe it or not, it is actually hard work being ourselves. We've got teachers and parents and employers and neighbors and important community members barking at us like tiny terriers. A closer look will reveal their expectations as nothing but a vague set of reasonless rules. Regardless of what started the cycle, we have the power. We can take a stand and explain that we will do what makes us happy. And that will be the end of it. They can accept us for who we are or they can leave.

IF YOU CAN FIND THE PEACE AND CLARITY TO ACCEPT WHERE YOU ARE, YOU WILL SOON HAVE THE INSIGHT TO GET WHERE YOU'D LIKE TO GO.

DON'T ASK FOR PERMISSION.

You've got people all around you explaining the rules and giving advice. They have many tiny suggestions. But what no one ever mentions is that sometimes trying something stupid can have the most extraordinary results. The days we ignore common sense are sometimes the days we can look back on when we're older and say, "Thank God I was bold that day."

They tell us that we'll never amount to
anything. They tell us to go back to
college. Get that MBA. They insist that
if we don't learn how to dress properly,
no one will ever take us seriously. They
dribble red wine on the floor and they spit
when they talk. The last time they saw a
sunset, it was by happenstance on the way
to a work meeting. The last time they felt
any passion in the bedroom was when they
drank too much at the country club. When
they look in the mirror, they don't see
themselves. They only see an image to be
groomed by the standards of others. They
have plenty of advice. And they're quite
happy to share it.

Sometimes it's okay to get angry. It's okay to stand on your own two feet and say to the world, "You're gonna have to accept me because I'm not leaving." Sometimes it's fine to shout out loud, let everybody know where you are and what you're thinking. Sometimes we've got no choice but to flaunt our stuff and show the world what we got.

Do you know how rare it is to be human? Do you know what a miracle it is to get all your energy wrapped up in that functioning body of yours? It'd take 30 lifetimes just to understand it all. You are a walking, talking, embodiment of the consciousness of our planet and your only job is to love. Love yourself and love the people around you. Love the air you breathe and love every person you ever meet – whether they appreciate it or not. That stuff has transforming powers and it is a double-edged sword of helpfulness. It will change your life and elevate the people around you.

The world doesn't want the same thing
all of the time. They want something
different. They want something honest and
new. Don't cheapen yourself. Stay weird.
If things feel boring or stale, do something
unexpected. Continue to reinvent yourself
and strive towards the extraordinary.

Inner values are there for you when everything else falls apart. If you're well centered and true to who you are, you'll be able to make helpful compromises in the external world and build some extraordinary things with amazing people.

People who change the world don't get wrapped up in today's fashions.

It's your mind. You can believe in God or physics or love at first sight. You can believe in telepathy or prayer or astral projection. No one around you knows anymore about these things than you do. Try different things and see what works. What makes you feel good? What feels right? Forget the experts. They used to think the earth was flat. If you think you can communicate with loved ones who have died or control your own future by maintaining a positive attitude, then you are absolutely correct.

When people tell you you love somebody too much, don't listen to them. When they tell you to forget about it, don't listen to them. When they tell you to let him or her go, try harder to win him or her back. If you love someone, there's a reason. These things aren't just "in your head." The urges are real. Your feelings are real.

BE THE CALM, CENTERED VERSION OF YOURSELF. THIS IS THE MOST PRODUCTIVE AND INSPIRING VERSION.

In school they teach us all to go after
the same things. They teach us how to
apply for the same jobs and how to compete
with each other. In school, they teach
us to avoid making mistakes. But mistakes
are honest and mistakes are beautiful and
mistakes are where insight comes from. What
they never teach us in school is that the
biggest rewards come from the biggest risks.
If millions of people go to a top tier
University to get their masters degree, the
value of said degree decreases. If hundreds
of people apply for the same job, the
employer is in a position to lower salaries
and cut benefits. When you play by the
rules, you will always be in second place
to the rule makers. In this day and age we
must burn our own paths. We must find a
creative solution and be honest with what
we're capable of accomplishing. It takes a
mindset that is okay with fumbling around
and learning how to be a leader. It takes
someone who understands that taking risks is
the only way to accomplish something great.

DON'T BE AFRAID TO DISREGARD THAT WHICH DOES NOT GET YOUR BLOOD BOILING IN THE MORNING.

There is no need to imitate what is popular.
We are all different for a reason. When
we push our inner thoughts aside in hopes
of winning approval – we lose touch with
ourselves. There's no reason for it. We
have plenty to offer just the way we are.

Embrace risk and wonderful things will
happen.

If you have a dream, if you have a love or
a talent you want to perfect - you've got
to be in charge of yourself. You can't look
to others for direction or approval. No
one cares. If you want to build the life
you envision, you've got to have a lot of
guts to go out there and do it your way.
It takes years of practice, but if you're
honest with yourself when challenges arise,
you'll find the power to rise above.

I think it's important for every person to
have some sort of creative outlet to express
themselves - especially those who aren't so
good at holding a conversation. Writing
works for me but try anything - hiking,
podcasting, cooking or fly-fishing. If
you can make a living from your creative
endeavors, that is great but by no means
necessary.

Don't let advertising agencies sell you
the idea that you need something outside
yourself to better your life. You are a
miracle.

BREAKING THE RULES CAN SOMETIMES TURN OUT REALLY WELL.

I believe in lifestyle design. I believe in embracing passions and focusing on the things we're good at. I'm all about accepting ourselves and being honest about what we want. So if I want to write books all night, I should be able to find a way to do that. If you want to throw out your cell phone and go live off the land, you should be able to go and do that. If you want to drop out of school and start a website about collecting vintage Zippos and spend your time restoring wicks and flints, what's stopping you?

Avoid those who always have comments or a critique about art or beauty or performance of any kind. Beware of people who are always talking. They lack wisdom and tend to miss the important things in life. Trust your gut. When you have a thought, don't push it aside. Listen to your intuition. And most importantly, when you think you are in love, you are.

Be unapologetic. And you will come to know
things about yourself that others only
sometimes catch glimpses of while they doze
off to sleep.

Art is personal and making art is selfish.
You have to be selfish when you make art.
If you're worried about what other people
will think, you're going to lose the truth.
You're going to break contact with the
muse. It will all fall apart. When you
are out and about and shaking hands in an
art gallery, fine. Make eye contact and
smile. Have meaningful discussions and
be the 'relatable and friendly' version of
yourself. But when you are in the honest
flow of self-expression, there is no room
for being polite. There is no room for
anything but you and the force that put you
here.

SOMETIMES EXTRAORDINARY AND EXCITING NEW GENRES OF MUSIC ARE INVENTED BY PEOPLE ON DRUGS WHO NEVER LEARNED HOW TO PROPERLY PLAY THEIR INSTRUMENTS.

Appear where no one else can appear. Create
things that no one has ever seen before.

The secret to all of this is sustainability.
Don't take a risk so big that you'll have
to call it quits. Always have a way to stay
in the game. The smartest thing you can do
with a record deal is to take the advance
and build a studio in your basement. That
way, if the first record doesn't do well and
you get dropped, you'll still have a studio
in your basement to record the next one.

One of the worst feelings is to not have
enough money in the bank to go out and start
a new project. That's why I cook at home
more often than eating out. It's why I
only own one pair of shoes and do not have
cable television. I read a book recently
in which the author argued that most people
never become rich because they get bored
too quickly. He claims that it takes years
of patience and sacrifices to build wealth.
It's imperative to stick to a financial
plan. But most people get bored too quickly
and move on to something else. They get
distracted. They look for quick and easy
solutions and fuck it up. I think the same
thing is true for art or lifestyle creation.
It's all about having an uncomplicated plan
and having the endurance to show up every
day and stick to the plan. You can't give
up just because your first book didn't make
the best-seller list.

THE MORE YOU FAIL, THE MORE CAPABLE YOU BECOME.

Here's a secret and this is a secret I
believe with every ounce of my soul - If you
don't succeed this time, you'll have double
the chance of succeeding next time. I
believe this to be true because when you are
learning something new, you are figuring out
how to finish it. You are making mistakes
and learning how to avoid them next time.
You're gaining insight on how to be more
efficient with your efforts. Once you know
how to do something once, you can do it
again and again and get better every time.

Whatever it is that you're trying to do with your life, whether it's getting a gallery show in Chelsea or finding investor funds for a full-length feature film, keep hope. Keep your hope safe. Keep it safe in a jar and put some holes in the top so it can breathe. Hide it in a place where mom and dad will never find it. Remember to feed and water it daily. If someone asks to borrow it, refuse. Change your hiding place often and play with your hope every day. If you take care of your hope, it will get stronger. And it will grow and you will need a bigger jar. And one day, your hope won't fit in a jar anymore. Your hope will be too strong to ignore. It will grow like a hot air balloon. And you will not want to hide it anymore. When hope is ready, you will sail into the skies with it - shooting giant roars of flames that are so hot they'll take you where you've always wanted to go.

Change is good. It can turn your strengths
into invincible powers. Sometimes you get
sick of sitting in the chair so you build
a standing desk. Sometimes you get bored
with painting so you dive into sculpture.
Whatever is happening in your world, don't
stop. Things will click and doors will
open. I believe in personal growth. But
compromising for something you're not
passionate about is not growth. Learning to
wear a tie and sell blenders to the buyers
of department stores is not growth.

How do you tell the difference between striving for growth and pretending to be something that you're not? Growth comes from facing fear. Pretending happens when you run from fear. Growth is something that comes after you do something that terrifies you. Pretending is when you never admit to yourself what you really wanted.

GO AFTER WHAT YOU WANT IN LIFE BECAUSE THE THINGS THAT SCARE US ARE DAMN TINY COMPARED TO THAT BASTARD CALLED DEATH.

I am messy. And I am emotional. I am
flawed but I strive to be the best version
of myself. I keep friends who accept every
part of me and I do the same for them. I
work in environments where I am allowed to
shine. I love souls who are in tune with
themselves and in love with the world.

Audacity and passion will always mean more to me than the ability to emulate the talents of others.

Individual expression and niche marketing
is the natural way of the world. Cramming
a one-size-fits-all product down people's
throats makes most people want to throw up.

Keep friends who inspire you - the ones who
have your best interests at heart. Let go
of those who bring you down. They will find
other people to annoy.

If you feel like you're in last place, get out and start your own game. If you feel like you have a chance, try harder. And if you're in first place, continue to reinvent yourself. You make the rules. Everything you see around you can be changed.

- Part Four -

CHALLENGES

Sometimes we face challenges in our lives. It's very easy to give up. It's very easy to quit. But the truth is that quitting sucks. If something is important to you and you quit, you may regret it one day. It's pretty hard to get started again after you quit. This chapter is about persevering when things get difficult. It's about rising to challenges and seeing things through. It's not always easy. But if you love something enough and believe that the task is important, quitting won't be an option. I believe we can do anything if we want it bad enough.

NO MATTER HOW MUCH YOU'VE FAILED OR SUCCEEDED THUS FAR, ALWAYS START EACH DAY WITH THE SAME PASSION AND FERVOR AS THE FIRST DAY.

If you feel stuck, sometimes the solution is to do the difficult thing. Don't take the easy way out. Explore the thing that you have never done before. You will grow stronger and more confident. You will get to know parts of yourself and acquire extraordinary abilities – new talents that can never be taken from you.

Facing challenges will give you confidence.
Start with something small. Do something
that scares you a little bit. Conquer it.
Up the stakes. Chase after challenges and
you will learn a great deal about yourself.

Sometimes you've really got to throw your weight into it to actually get things done. Don't be afraid to do that.

It doesn't matter what you attempt. It doesn't matter if you fail. It doesn't matter if you go bankrupt or break a bone. You will heal and you will smile again. And your next meal will taste better and your next orgasm will wake the neighbors because you are free and you ran towards the thing that scared you most and you came out on the other side - maybe limping but smiling and more alive than you've felt in a very long time.

We've got to really love what we're doing
if we hope to make a life out of it. The
closer we get to our goals, the less sexy
they become. The higher we get to the
top, the more the glamour fades. After we
accomplish something big, it doesn't feel so
glorious or special or even that difficult.
This is why we must love the craft itself.
We should burn our ideal resume and really
fall in love with the day-to-day.

If things aren't happening for you, if you get bored, find a way to rekindle the interest and push yourself in new and exciting ways. Don't walk away. Push through the boredom and fall in love with your craft again.

You will get bored and you will get
discouraged and you will look like a real
jack ass from time to time. But if you
quit, it's all over. If you stop or reach
so far that you lose your balance, the whole
thing will be destroyed. Chip away, dear
friend. Tiny victories will lead you to
where you need to be.

Problems will come every day. No matter what you do, you will have problems. You could win the lottery, quit your job and live on a beach with a supermodel. You'd still have problems. They never go away. What matters is your ability to overcome. Have inner strength deep enough to keep your feet firmly planted in the sand when the ocean tries to wash you away.

SHIT IS HARD.
DO IT ANYWAY.

Everybody wants to give up. Everyone has doubts. I want to give up. The most successful and prolific people in the world want to give up. But they don't surrender. They get their shit together and keep going.

The excitement will wear off. It will become more appealing to abandon what you started and run after something new. This is the point that determines your success or failure. You have to push through those struggles and refuse to give up. Refuse. People say, "Don't give up" all the time. People say it so much that it has begun to loose it's meaning. People post quotes on Instagram and we all skim past them. But this one is real. Don't give up. If you quit, it's going to change you. If you allow other people or outside circumstances to convince you that you can't do something, you're going to turn into a sad fucker.

This isn't supposed to be easy. It's like learning how to walk. And when you were a child, learning to walk was like learning to fly. It was another dimension of existence - your head and your arms flying around up there, it felt unnatural. But you kept trying and now it's no problem. New endeavors are much easier than learning how to walk.

Go climb that rock wall at the gym, join the flying trapeze school or finally record one of those songs you wrote and post it online for the world to hear. I promise you that if you do it once, you will have the power to do it again and again and get better than you ever imagined.

It's all a game. It's a fun game. Find a part of the game that you enjoy. Play with it and get better. Move to the next level. Play with better players. Win sometimes. Lose sometimes. Years will pass and you will become a pro without realizing it has happened. The changes over the years will be so subtle. You play because it is fun. You won't lose as often as you used to. Some people will say you are the best. You don't care. You just like to play.

Once you get the first thing done, your life will open up. You'll learn that language and make time for traveling and you'll conquer that fear of public speaking and quit that dirty habit of yours. The inner confidence will grow and expand and you will inspire people around you.

Be brave. That fear you're feeling won't kill you. It is completely natural and many other people feel it every day. If you can learn to sit in that fear – to feel it and move forward anyway, the world's biggest doors will open for you. All your idols live with that fear just as much as you do. We are all in this together. We all get nervous. We think we're no good and we want to turn back. But a few crazy people lean into the fear. They learn to function in the fear. And if you can adopt that as a permanent outlook, you will get every last drop out of this gift called life.

Dreams are not meant to be delayed. They should not be left to chance. Your plan for the future should not be "hope." Dreams are the desired outcome from specific actionable steps. Every grandiose fantasy can be broken down into smaller goals. Move towards them as quickly as possible. Jump.

It doesn't matter what's happening
right now. You might be failing in all
directions. That stuff doesn't matter.
What matters is whether or not you can see a
way to succeed. If you have a plan that you
know will work, focus on that plan.

It might not be easy. But if your desire is strong enough, you'll accomplish what you set out to do.

Rising to a big challenge and accomplishing something extraordinary happens by diligently and consistently getting tiny bits of work done. It is about working within your skill level and ability and never stretching yourself to the point of breaking. You will improve daily if you practice daily. And you will appear to be an overnight success after thousands of hours of hard work.

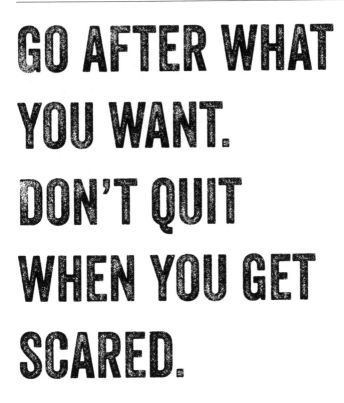

GO AFTER WHAT YOU WANT. DON'T QUIT WHEN YOU GET SCARED.

Humans don't like uncertainty. It is the most terrifying thing in our lives. It's why we invented religions. Uncertainty breeds fear and conflict and racism and greed and war and all the small-minded, stupid things we do. We are human and we want to feel secure. But extraordinary things come from the unknown. Maybe you don't know where you're going or how you'll get there. And maybe you'll end up on a completely different and unexpected planet. But don't give up. Don't shut the thing down. Once you leave the house and you start your run, don't turn back. Have faith in the thing that brought you here and be brave enough to see it through to the end.

There is no need for pressure. We should be operating from a place of peace and balance. We are successful because we are aligned with our goals and capabilities. We take actions that optimize results. We rest and find peace in order to conserve our energy. We strike before our opponents even know what's happening.

High pressure is a poison. It can cripple
you. But the thing about poisons is that
we can become immune to them. Once there
was a man named Bill Haast. He owned a
Serpentarium, a vicious and deadly place
filled with poisonous snakes. Bill took a
chance and started injecting himself with
snake venom. Every week he increased the
dosage. Years went by and he survived
172 snake bites and lived to be 100 years
old. He donated his blood to be used as an
anti-venom. High pressure situations are a
lot like this. They can destroy us. They
can kill your career and stop you dead in
your tracks if you make a mistake. But if
you stretch yourself out of your comfort
zone, if you push yourself just a little
more each day, you will become unstoppable.
Eventually, years will pass and you'll be so
hopped up on deadly fang juice that nothing
can kill you.

The pain is too much to go on but we push ourselves anyway. Because to stop here would just be a depressing ending and we would rather die on our way to the top then quit one day too soon.

Your outlook will change. Your mindset will evolve. Most likely, even your friends and love interests will transform. As Einstein said, "No problem can be solved from the same level of consciousness that created it."

Those who seek out challenges and growth, shall be well equipped for future spiritual battles and interpersonal attacks.

There isn't time to look for sympathy, approval or adoration. We must have unwavering courage within ourselves.

You do not need to be brutal - only
consistent. Keep showing up. Keep trying.

You don't need everything to go your way.
In fact, you can fuck up most of the time
and still accomplish your goals if you keep
showing up.

I was watching one of those TV shows recently about people who live in Alaska. And there was this scene where a rancher was trying to get his cattle to cross a river. But rain had just come and the river was flowing higher and faster than usual. The rancher said, "Well, if we try here and the cattle get spooked, they wont go near water again even if we find a nice shallow spot." The rancher prevented the cattle from developing a fearful association with that river. This is why small wins and seeking out small challenges is important. If you're finding little obstacles and overcoming them, you're developing a positive mindset and a belief in yourself. So when a small-sized challenge presents itself you jump right in without being afraid. And eventually, you graduate to medium-sized challenges. And then one day, you're doing the back stroke with a bunch of cows and not even thinking about it.

Raise your standards and refuse to go lower than that. Believe anything is possible and it will be.

We need to be very specific about our goals.
You can't try and put a round peg in a
square hole. Let's not get mad at the world
because the thing we want isn't working.
Let's find a way to make it work. Let's
think about what's most important and not
stop until we get there.

Be careful about what you're good at. Stay the course that leads you where you want to go.

Let's hold our ground. Not just once, let's refuse to take no for an answer every time until we succeed. If we refuse to fail, there is no other option. People will get out of the way eventually.

Experience is the second most valuable thing in your favor. Build it up. Build a track record and a history. Make mistakes so that you're well informed. Learn things that you won't forget. Experience is the second most helpful asset while facing a challenge. The most valuable thing is GUTS.

Sometimes the best way to succeed is to welcome the possibility of failure right into your living room. Sometimes the best way to learn to fly is to jump from very high places without any sort of guarantee. We can do extraordinary things when the consequences of failure are just too serious to mess with.

We're going to make mistakes and say stupid things. Don't get down on yourself. There are hundreds of people out there who are more than happy to do this for you. Let other people worry about your failures. Let other people worry about all those times you were an idiot. All you need to do is focus on what can be and keep moving towards that happy place.

Sometimes our dreams can appear like some
kind of giant mountain. We have no idea
how we're going to get to the top. But
people have been up there before. They left
little clues. Their foot prints and ropes
are still up there. Those people are not
luckier than you are. They made mistakes
and came close to falling just like anyone
would. But they made it. And so will you.

Let us not be discouraged. Let us find peace and start again.

- Part Five -

There is something extremely dangerous about doing things alone. It's foolish. When we refuse to listen, we are causing harm to ourselves. We are running the engines hot without a map. Every great talent was surrounded by a support team of teachers, advisors, mentors, lovers and family. Solo success is an illusion. When it comes to great accomplishments, we must ask for help.

There are groups of seekers out there —
natural born teachers offering guidance,
passion and information. Find them.
Embrace what you don't know and keep your
ear to the ground. It's only when we
realize that we don't know much, that we
really start to grow.

Look to those that are successful in the
thing you are interested in. If you want
to learn about inner peace and meditation,
go to a zen center. If you want to write
books, have lunch with a published writer.
If you want to make a million dollars, get
a millionaire on the phone. If you want to
start a charity, schedule a meeting with
someone who has done it before. Listen.
Pay attention.

It takes guts to admit when you don't know something. It takes courage to reach out to someone and say, "I want to learn about what you do. Will you teach me?"

It's okay to feel like you're out of your
league. If you feel capable and comfortable,
you've probably been there too long already.

Keep people who inspire you in your life.
Seek teachers and study great artists. No
matter how talented or gifted you are,
you've had a long line of great people come
before you. Learn from them.

I have many mentors. There will always people who know more than me. There will always be people with more experience, more success, more money, maybe even more happiness. I find it best to know these people and to learn from them.

SURROUND YOURSELF WILL PEOPLE WHO ARE EXCITED BY THE THRILL OF A TALL CHALLENGE. RUN WITH A CROWD THAT BELIEVES THEY CAN FLY.

One strange lesson that stuck out to me while I was in school was this phenomenon I learned about in management class. It was about the optimal number of people working together. It defies all logic. If Worker A alone can produce 2 units an hour and Worker B alone can produce 2 units alone, then together they can produce 4 units, right? No. This assumption is false when it comes to human beings. When people work together, they're able to accomplish more. Sometimes 2+2=5. This is a proven fact. Together we can defy the laws of mathematics and accomplish the impossible.

If something isn't working, change it. Be openminded to the terrifying possibility that you don't know everything.

One of my business heros was on TV the
other day. He was helping this skateboard
company with marketing advice. And I'll
paraphrase this but basically he was saying,
"Listen this business is very straight
forward. You don't have to build a market
from scratch. You sell to the people that
buy skateboards." And that really struck me
because as artists, we all want to be one-
of-a-kind. We all want to be innovators.
And that's fine and good and everything.
But the simple fact remains that there is
a pre-existsing marketplace and a long line
of inspiring souls who have come before us.
We'd be goddamned fools if we didn't take
their advice.

Once you've learned how to cultivate the guts to keep moving forward, once you're no longer threatened by the possibility of being wrong, then the world becomes a playground and doors will open that you never knew existed. Entire cities will reveal themselves and yesterdays dreams will seem so tiny compared to what you now know is possible.

Mentors are invaluable. When you are talking with someone who has done what you want to do, and they are looking at you like they believe there's every chance in the world you will accomplish the same thing, it can have a very positive effect on your life.

It's important to note that we should never put "needy" energy into the world. Yes, we can seek out professionals for guidance. But it's up to us to do the work. Nothing shuts the door quicker than a "needy" question or a whiny tone of voice screeching in the universe. Start with gratitude for what you have. Give what you have. Come from a place of giving – giving everything you have inside you. You must offer every last drop of energy and then slowly it comes back to you and you are re-born.

VOLUNTEERING IS A HOT SHOWER FOR THE SOUL.

If you've ever accomplished something noteworthy, if you've got secret talents or knowledge that could help somebody, give it away. Send it out into the world and see what it brings back. And if you're just starting out, have faith in the fact that you are not alone. People are helpful and generous and most of them are kind enough to make themselves available to you.

Yes, we compete but it's a lot more fun
when we help each other become better
competitors. It's more fun when we
challenge each other, push each other. Tell
everyone your greatest secrets and give your
power away. It grows a little every time
you let it go.

Teach. When you share what you know, you reinforce your skills and knowledge and stretch yourself to get better. I learned this phenomenon many years ago when I was still in high school. I was taking drum lessons and my teacher said something about HIS teacher. And I said, "You still take drum lessons?" And he said, "Yeah, dude, you're never too good to stop learning." So there was my drum teacher still learning and improving every week. And I was sucking up every last bit of knowledge. Shortly after that, I became the section leader of my school's drum line and started to play the role of teacher myself. We are never at a point where we can stop learning. Even if you haven't been playing for so long, you can always help and teach others. To be a student and a teacher at once is to truly be immersed in your subject.

Once you've found the craft you love and you start to get some momentum, share it with other people. Teach that thing you love so that other's can love it too. When you give, you will always benefit. If embraced, this principal will transform your life.

Writing has helped me immensely. I find that when I think out loud and put ideas on paper, I learn what works and what doesn't. When I share my ideas, it makes me want to learn more so that I have more to offer. I didn't know what I was doing when I first started. But things came together. I feel wiser than I did when I first started.

I have many people I consider mentors. Some of them I have actually asked, "Will you mentor me?" and we've agreed to this type of relationship. Other's are more casual - writers or investors that I feel very comfortable emailing to ask for advice. Some people I consider mentors even though I don't think they realize I think of them this way. I still learn from them. And I try to offer help back to people however I can. I always try to be as helpful as possible when other people look to me for guidance. I always try to pass the little knowledge I have on to the next guy. This book is an attempt at that.

We can't do everything ourselves. The best
we can ask for is to be decent at one or two
things and to have a great team of experts
around us. The quicker we learn to partner
up and trust our community, the quicker
we'll realize how lucky we are and how easy
and wonderful life can be with the right
people in our life.

I am pretty much terrible at almost
everything. I don't know anything about
marketing. I'm not very personable. I'm
a terrible public speaker. I'm bad at
sports. I'm not a very good driver. I
don't take direction well. But I am a very
small piece in a large puzzle and I know
my strengths. We all work together. We
let each other shine. We respect each
other's talents and help each other whenever
possible. I play one part in a large group
of artists, musicians, lawyers, publicists,
financial advisors, mentors, friends,
neighbors, investors, farmers, store
owners, publishers, printers and typewriter
repairmen. I only have one small thing to
offer and I do it humbly and gratefully. I
write.

I learned a great deal from growing up in
punk rock bands. As much as we appear to be
dirty, anti-social and unapproachable, the
truth is that community played a great deal
in our culture. Punk rockers take care of
each other. Many of us were rejected in
other areas of our lives. We came together
because there was no where else to go. And
we found a place where we could express
ourselves and all our strange tendencies.
We accepted and encouraged each other.
Sure, we got into fist fights once in a
while but we always picked each other up
when somebody fell down in the pit.

WE CAN ACCOMPLISH MORE TOGETHER.

My friend and I were at a Met's game the other day. And we were talking about the music industry like we sometimes do (he works with some of the biggest bands in the world). We were sitting there and he happened to say, "I'm still growing. There's still a lot I can learn." And I felt proud to be his friend right then. Power can be a hot thing to hold and it can turn people sour. But my friend is a wise one. People like him are constantly improving, giving back and expanding their capabilities. When we start each day like beginners, we always learn something new.

Having people in your life and being part
of some kind of community is the point of
all of this. But you can find insight and
guidance in other resources as well. Spend
a day at the book store and fill your
arms with the worlds greatest knowledge.
Don't feel guilty about spending money on
education. Just because there's no degree
at the end, doesn't mean it's not worth
every penny. Some people love seminars.
Other's like online courses or webinars.
I'm an audio guy. I've always got podcasts
going in my office. And I love books.
Thousands of books with everything I've
ever wanted to know. Embrace the lifestyle
of continued education and you will never
stagnate.

Those who get it right on the first try will
have myths and movies written about them.
The rest of us have to live in the real
world and stumble a bit before we get there.
The rest of us actually have to work on
ourselves and our abilities before we have
the tools needed to succeed.

I am reading constantly. If I am struggling
with something or stumble upon something
I don't understand, I seek help. I do
research and ask questions. I used to
stubbornly try to push through on my
own. Years have taught me that this is
almost always a mistake. There are experts
in every field and it's usually best to
approach things as a beginner. Seek the
counsel and expertise of those who have been
there before you.

If you don't know, ask.

Truly successful artists are some of the geekiest fans in their industries. They love the great innovators that have come before them. They know the heritage and the long-line of cultural ancestors that have paved the way. They fill the role because they do not take it lightly. And those who approach their art too recklessly do not last.

Learn the rules before you go around
breaking everything.

You don't have to be a follower. But you
should know the whole story before you make
a decision. You should know where the path
is headed before you go your own way.

Sometimes I pretend that I am living the same life over and over again. There is no death, there is just here and now over and over again. I am nice to people because it makes me happy. I might as well, I'm gonna have to live this moment over and over again. My whole life I'll have to repeat it for eternity. Might as well keep the good vibes going. I try to help people and not be selfish. Being selfish is restrictive. It makes me small. It makes my soul clench up. And since I'm gonna be living these days over and over and over again, I might as well give and give and give and try to create good vibes around me.

Let us give our money to people who deserve it. Let us dedicate our time and use our greatest talents to help others. Let us live by example and challenge ourselves. Let us grow stronger, not for ourselves but because we are intertwined with the people around us and want to see them succeed.

Whether we'd like to admit it or not, we
are role models. People will look to us.
And they will imitate us for better or
worse. So the next time you're thinking
about letting some darkness into your life,
reconsider the fact that the people around
you may try the same.

I try to live my live like an open book.
I try not to hold anything back because
I find that when I do that, I get stuck
with negative things that simmer. It's
better to let everything out there in art
or sex or late night conversations that
turn into early morning hugs. And when the
vulnerability and imperfections spill out,
we can pick them up off the floor in the
early morning light and get a good look at
them.

I would like to thank all of the people who
helped me become the person I am today. I
would like to thank all the people who
give back, all the people who accomplished
incredible things and taught others to do
the same. I would like to thank the people
who volunteered their time. Without these
wonderful souls, the human race would be
nothing but jackals.

In my first publication, I wrote that
right now is a very incredible time to be
alive. We are all very lucky to live in
this time in history. It's the information
age. Everything you ever wanted to know
is available to you. Would you like to
publish a book? It's easy. Would you like
to make a million dollars in real estate?
The information is there. Dating? A happy
marriage? Building a log cabin by hand?
There are people out there - people who have
been through what you're going through –
people who have accomplished great feats.
And a lot of them are reachable. A lot of
them are willing to teach you if you ask the
right questions. Believe you can and you
will.

CONCLUSION.

I started writing to help other people create art and build businesses. And I've said all I have to say about that. In a few years, writing these books has helped me in my life immensely. And I believe these ideas will transform your life as well if you apply them. But it's up to you now. It's up to you to put them into action. Find a mentor, start a zine. Move fast and follow the people who have already gone where you wish to go.

If you need anything, I'll be here: brooklyntomars@gmail.com.

I would like to thank my high school band director for making me section leader and instilling a tiny sense of self-confidence in me when I needed it most. I would like to thank my father for driving me to drum lessons in the first place and for waiting in the car even in the dead of winter. And I would like to thank singers and poets and mad genius lunatics who paved a path for starry-eyed loners to crawl towards. And I'd like to thank the millionaires and best-selling authors for returning my emails after I begged them repeatedly for advice. I'd like to thank my mother for being a stay-at-home mom and for teaching me how to read. I'd like to thank my

wife for unconditional love and for sticking
with me even during my dark times. I'd like
to thank New York bookstores. And I'd like to
thank you. Thank you for reading this. Thank
you for giving me a chance. Thank you for
everything.

-Markus Almond

P.S. If you enjoyed this book, check out
"Brooklyn To Mars: Volume One." It's about
starting where you are and going someplace
extraordinary.

OTHER BOOKS BY MARKUS ALMOND:

Brooklyn To Mars: Volume One

Things To Shout Out Loud At Parties

This Book Will Break A Window If You Throw
It Hard Enough

Marching Band and the Expanding Universe

Made in the USA
San Bernardino, CA
01 December 2016